ONE-MINUTE SPORTS DEVOTIONS
FOR YOUNG ATHLETES

BIBLICAL GUIDANCE FOR TEENS TO BUILD MENTAL TOUGHNESS, DISCIPLINE, AND A GROWTH MINDSET

RISE UP SPORTS

One-Minute Sports Devotions for Young Athletes: Biblical Guidance for Teens to Build Mental Toughness, Discipline, and a Growth Mindset

All Scripture quotations, unless otherwise indicated, are taken from the Holy Bible, New International Version®, NIV®. Copyright © 1973, 1978, 1984, 2011 by Biblica, Inc.™ Used by permission of Zondervan. All rights reserved worldwide.
www.zondervan.com

The "NIV" and "New International Version" are trademarks registered in the United States Patent and Trademark Office by Biblica, Inc.™

The real-life sports stories in this devotional are based on widely known events, public interviews, and publicly available information. Every effort has been made to ensure accuracy. Any direct quotes have been properly attributed. This book is not affiliated with or endorsed by any of the athletes mentioned.

Rise Up Sports publishes its books in both electronic and print formats. Please note that certain content may be included in the print version but not in the electronic edition, and vice versa.

This book is intended for devotional and inspirational purposes and should not be used as a substitute for professional theological, legal, or counseling advice.

CONTENTS

THE GAME PLAN

Talent will only take you so far. The best athletes know that success takes more—discipline, mental toughness, and a drive to keep pushing when it gets hard.

Kurt Warner stocked grocery shelves before becoming a Hall of Fame quarterback. Jeremy Lin rode the bench before the world knew his name. Albert Pujols? Overlooked before he became one of baseball's greatest hitters. What do they have in common? Faith. It's what kept them going when the odds were stacked against them.

For the next 40 days, you'll dig into stories of faith and sports—the highs, the struggles, and the moments that shape who you become. Here's what you'll find each day:

Bible Verse – A daily verse sets the theme for each devotion.

Lessons from the Game – Real stories from athletes that connect to biblical wisdom.

Putting It into Play – A challenge to help you apply what you've learned.

Prayer – A short prayer to refocus your heart and mind.

You train hard to grow as an athlete—what if you trained your faith with some of that same energy?

Small, consistent reps in Scripture and prayer will develop you, not just in sports, but as a leader, teammate, and person.

Stay committed. Put in the work. That's how real growth happens.

01

EXCELLENCE FOR HIS GLORY

Not to us, LORD, not to us but to your name be the glory,
because of your love and faithfulness.
Psalm 115:1

LESSONS FROM THE GAME

When the spotlight's on you, what will you do with it?

In the 2024 College Football Playoff National Championship, Ohio State quarterback Will Howard had just led his team to the biggest win of his life—a hard-fought victory over Notre Dame. The stadium exploded with cheers. Cameras swarmed. Reporters rushed the field, ready for their soundbite from the night's biggest star.

This was Howard's moment. After hundreds of hours in the weight room, watching film, and perfecting his game on the field, he could have made it about himself. But that's not what he did.

With adrenaline still pumping and emotions running high, his first words were: "I've got to give the glory and the praise to my Lord and Savior Jesus Christ... I wouldn't be here without Him, I wouldn't be here without my teammates, without my family... I'm at a loss for words right now."

At the biggest moment of his career, Howard didn't take the credit. He redirected it—to God, his teammates, and his family.

Psalm 115:1 reminds us that our talents and victories aren't just for us—they're meant to glorify God. The world defines excellence by achievements. But true excellence is measured by who you reflect when the spotlight is on you.

True excellence is also about how you treat teammates, respect opponents, handle bad calls, and stay humble through wins and losses. It's in the effort you give when no one's watching—when there's no crowd or cameras.

Your skills, your success—those are gifts. How you use them says everything about what matters most to you.

At the end of the day, true greatness shines brightest when it reflects God's glory, not our own.

PUTTING IT INTO PLAY

This week, find ways to shift the spotlight off yourself. You may not have a post-game interview like Will Howard, but you can still redirect attention in everyday moments. Try celebrating a teammate's success or giving credit to those who helped you improve.

PRAYER

Dear Lord, when the spotlight is on me, help me turn it back to You. May my actions, words, and attitude bring You glory, on and off the field. Please help me remember that true excellence isn't about recognition but about who I reflect. Let me celebrate others, stay humble, and always point back to You. Amen.

02

SHARP LIKE IRON

As iron sharpens iron, so one person sharpens another.
Proverbs 27:17

LESSONS FROM THE GAME

The best athletes don't just excel at their sport—they inspire higher standards for everyone around them.

Teammates play a huge role in our growth. Through practices, workouts, and competition, they push us to improve and reach our full potential. When one teammate gets better, the whole team rises, creating a cycle of growth that benefits everyone.

Look at the 2011-12 Kentucky Wildcats, one of the most talented rosters in college basketball history. That year, hundreds of fans filled the stands during their preseason practices, eager to watch a team so deep in talent. The Wildcats' roster featured seven future NBA players, including 10-time NBA All-Star Anthony Davis.

These players challenged one another daily, pushing each other's limits and demanding excellence. Giving less than your best wasn't an option. That competitive edge fueled their success, leading them to a national championship victory over Kansas that season.

Proverbs 27:17 says, "As iron sharpens iron, so one person sharpens another." The Wildcats embodied this, pushing each other to improve every day. But the idea that growth comes through challenge isn't new—it's a principle that has stood the test of time.

In ancient times, blacksmiths would sharpen iron blades by rubbing them together. The friction removed dull edges, making the blades sharper and more effective. That's what the right people do for us—they help shape our character and faith.

Just like a team needs players who push each other to improve, we need friends who help us grow spiritually. Surround yourself with people who encourage you, hold you accountable, and make you stronger in your walk with God. And just as others sharpen you, be the kind of person who sharpens those around you.

PUTTING IT INTO PLAY

Is your circle of friends helping you move closer to God or farther away from Him? Do they motivate you to become a better version of yourself? How can you actively help "sharpen" your friends?

PRAYER

Dear God, please guide me to invest in relationships that challenge me to grow in faith and become a better version of myself. Help me be a positive influence and sharpen those around me. Amen.

03

SET THE STANDARD

*Live such good lives among the pagans that, though they accuse
you of doing wrong, they may see your good deeds and glorify God
on the day he visits us.*
1 Peter 2:12

LESSONS FROM THE GAME

Tim Tebow wasn't just one of the greatest quarterbacks in college football history—he was also a game-changer off the field.

As a freshman backup quarterback, Tebow played a crucial role in the Florida Gators' 2006 national championship, stepping in for high-pressure goal-line situations to help punch the ball into the end zone. As the starter from 2007 to 2009, he dominated, winning the Heisman Trophy and leading the Gators to another National Championship in 2008.

However, what truly set Tebow apart wasn't just his ability to bulldoze through defenders or launch a rocket downfield. It was his unwavering commitment to his Christian faith.

Tebow was one of the most outspoken Christians in college sports, while some of his teammates were known for partying and legal trouble. In fact, during his 2008 championship season, nearly a third of the team was arrested. While some teammates were out getting into trouble, Tebow was in hospitals visiting sick children and leading team Bible studies. The contrast was undeniable.

But Tebow's passion for sharing the Gospel and helping others earned the respect of his teammates, even those who didn't share his faith. His humility inspired them to give back, and while not all embraced his faith, they all experienced the love of Jesus through him.

Being a Christian on a team where not everyone shares your faith can be challenging. But like Tebow, see it as an opportunity to stand out in a positive way and share God's love. In 1 Peter 2:12, we're encouraged to live in a way that helps others see God through us.

Living out your faith around those who don't share your beliefs isn't about being perfect or pushing your views onto them. It's about creating moments that could make them curious about the peace and joy that come from knowing Christ.

PUTTING IT INTO PLAY

How can you live out your faith with your team? Consider how your actions might speak louder than words. Remember, your example could be the very thing that helps someone see God in a new way.

PRAYER

Heavenly Father, thank You for the opportunity
to serve as Your representative on my team. Please
help me bring Your truth to others through the way
I live. Let my actions reflect Your love and draw my
teammates closer to You. Amen.

04

FROM TRIALS TO TRIUMPH

Not only so, but we also glory in our sufferings, because we know
that suffering produces perseverance; perseverance, character;
and character, hope.
Romans 5:3-4

LESSONS FROM THE GAME

Lopez Lomong's story has all the makings of a big-screen movie.

At just six years old, Lomong was kidnapped from his African village during the Sudanese Civil War. After a daring escape, he found himself in a Kenyan refugee camp—alone in a foreign country with no idea what his future held. With no way to contact his family and nothing but the clothes on his back, he made the camp his home for the next 10 years.

Through those years, Lomong's faith kept him going. Catholic missionaries in the refugee camp encouraged him to trust that God had a plan for his life. That belief gave him strength as he faced daily struggles.

The boys in the camp loved soccer, but younger players had to run an 18-mile lap just to earn a spot in the game. Determined to play, Lomong ran the long laps, never realizing he was building the endurance that would one day help make him a world-class runner.

After a decade in the refugee camp, Lomong's life took a dramatic turn—a Christian family in Upstate New York adopted him. Stepping onto a track for the first time in high school, his raw speed stunned coaches and competitors alike. He quickly became a standout, leading his team to multiple state titles in cross country and track. His dedication and faith carried him through a successful college career, and eventually, two Olympic appearances as a middle-distance runner.

Lomong's journey proves that struggles aren't setbacks—they're preparation. The hardships he faced in the refugee camp weren't just obstacles—they were the training ground for his future success. Like Lomong, we may not always understand our difficulties, but we can trust that God is using them to strengthen our character and equip us for what's ahead.

PUTTING IT INTO PLAY

What's a recent setback you've experienced? Instead of focusing on the disappointment, ask God to help you see how this situation can help you grow. Use this challenge as an opportunity to build strength and perseverance.

PRAYER

Dear God, thank You for walking with me through difficult times and showing me perseverance builds strength and hope. Help me see how You can use my struggles to grow my faith. Teach me to trust Your plan and remind me that I can face any challenge with You. Amen.

05

HUMBLE IN THE SPOTLIGHT

Humble yourselves before the Lord, and he will lift you up.
James 4:10

LESSONS FROM THE GAME

NBA superstar Giannis Antetokounmpo earned his nickname "The Greek Freak" for good reason—at 6'11" tall with freakish athleticism, he's nearly unstoppable on the court.

But what really sets him apart isn't his power on the court—it's his humility.

Antetokounmpo wasn't always a basketball phenom. Before the fame, he was just a kid in Greece, the son of Nigerian immigrants barely scraping by. His family often struggled to afford rent or put food on the table, and at one point, he and his brother had to share a single pair of basketball shoes—trading them off every time one subbed into a game. Everyone in his family pitched in, working whatever jobs they could to keep their household afloat.

Those early struggles shaped him. Growing up, Antetokounmpo didn't know where his next meal would come from. Fast forward a few years, and he was signing NBA contracts worth millions. But money didn't change him—the humility forged in those early hardships stayed with him, no matter how high he climbed.

While leading the Milwaukee Bucks to their first NBA championship in 50 years and being named Finals MVP in 2021, he was asked how he stays so humble when other young superstars let fame get to their heads. His response? "When you focus on the past, that's your ego... When I focus on the future, it's my pride... I try to focus... in the moment, in the present. That's humility."

Antetokounmpo understands that dwelling on past achievements can make us arrogant, and focusing too much on future success can make us prideful. Both can pull us away from what matters—being faithful and present in the moment.

His mindset exemplifies James 4:10: "Humble yourselves before the Lord, and He will lift you up." Success may come and go, but humility keeps us grounded in God's purpose.

Humility isn't about thinking less of yourself—it's about thinking of yourself less. It's recognizing that everything we have is a gift from God. The more we stay grounded, the more we grow into who He's calling us to be.

PUTTING IT INTO PLAY

What's something you're really proud of? Take a moment to thank God for whatever that is. Look for one opportunity today to put others first—whether it's giving someone credit or thanking someone for their help.

PRAYER

Dear Lord, please help me remember that all my success comes through You. Teach me to remain grounded and focused on the present, not my achievements. Remind me that true success isn't about status, but about walking faithfully with You. Amen.

06

TRUST THE PROCESS

*But seek first his kingdom and his righteousness,
and all these things will be given to you as well.*
Matthew 6:33

LESSONS FROM THE GAME

Oftentimes, the outcome of a game, race, or season can overshadow the process. While results are important, they can distract us from the daily effort and growth that lead to success.

Matthew 6:33 calls us to put God first and trust Him with the results. This doesn't mean results don't matter. It means that when we focus on doing what's right and prioritize God in our lives, He will take care of the rest, blessing us and providing what we need.

Albert Pujols, one of baseball's all-time greats, lived out this verse throughout his extraordinary MLB career. Drafted in the 13th round—an afterthought to many—

Pujols focused on hard work and faith instead of chasing fame or worrying about the odds.

Pujols always said baseball wasn't his true purpose: "My life is not mostly dedicated to the Lord, it is 100% committed to Jesus Christ and His will... But baseball is not the end; baseball is the means by which I glorify God."

This mindset led to incredible success. Pujols won three MVP awards, hit over 700 home runs, and earned two World Series titles over two decades—proving that focusing on the process rather than just the results brings lasting success.

Much like athletes commit to training habits to build strength, endurance, and skill, our faith grows through consistent spiritual practices. Daily prayer, reading Scripture, and serving others might not always seem exciting, but they lay the foundation for a fulfilling life. These are the practices that help us keep God a priority in our lives.

By trusting God in every step, we unlock His purpose for our lives and experience the peace that comes from knowing He's in control.

PUTTING IT INTO PLAY

This week, trust the process and focus on your effort rather than the end result. Ask yourself how you can value each step, knowing God's plan is unfolding through your commitment.

PRAYER

Dear God, thank You for teaching me that the process matters just as much as the final result. Help me put You first in my life and trust You with the outcome. May I find joy in the journey and grow through each step. Amen.

07

FINDING FULFILLMENT

*What good is it for someone to gain the
whole world, yet forfeit their soul?*
Mark 8:36

LESSONS FROM THE GAME

What if everything you thought defined success turned out to be empty?

As competitors, it's easy to believe that being the best will make us happy. But what happens when the trophies collect dust or the crowds stop cheering? If your whole identity is based only on sports, you might still feel empty, even if you've reached the highest levels of success.

Few athletes understand this better than Manny "Pacman" Pacquiao.

Pacquiao, a champion boxer with 12 world title wins, is celebrated as one of the greatest fighters in history. Known for his lightning-fast punches and ability to overwhelm opponents with speed and precision, he earned global fame and wealth throughout his legendary career.

But despite his success in the ring, Pacquiao admitted that he still felt empty inside. Outside of the boxing spotlight, he struggled with gambling, partying, and poor choices as he searched for something that could bring him true happiness.

Then everything changed. After a powerful encounter with God, Pacquiao realized that true fulfillment didn't come from titles, big houses, fancy cars, or fame. It came from a relationship with God. He gave his heart to Jesus, and his perspective shifted. Today, he shares how his faith has given him peace, purpose, and joy that no championship ever could.

Mark 8:36 warns that gaining everything in the world means nothing if you lose your soul. Time and time again, athletes and celebrities find that fame and material things don't bring lasting happiness.

True peace and joy aren't found in awards or achievements—they come from a relationship with God, who gives us purpose beyond what the world offers.

PUTTING IT INTO PLAY

What gives you your sense of worth? Is it your wins and accomplishments or your relationship with God? How can you make God more of a priority in your life?

PRAYER

Dear God, thank You for showing me that true fulfillment comes from You, not winning or fame. Please help me build my identity in You. Guide me to use every success as a way to uplift Your name. Amen.

08

DISCIPLINE OVER DISTRACTION

The prudent see danger and take refuge,
but the simple keep going and pay the penalty.
Proverbs 22:3

LESSONS FROM THE GAME

Talent can open doors, but discipline is what keeps them open.

Reaching the next level in your sport isn't just about natural skill—it's about discipline, smart decisions, and steering clear of anything that can slow you down.

Proverbs 22:3 teaches that wise people recognize and avoid danger, while others who fail to do so make poor choices and face the consequences. Professional basketball player A.C. Green's life shows us the importance of making wise decisions and avoiding distractions.

Known as the NBA's "Iron Man," Green played in a record 1,192 games in a row over 16 seasons, showing incredible strength and durability. But how did he do it? And is it a coincidence that one of the NBA's toughest players avoided drugs, alcohol, and smoking?

Green was a strong Christian known for his commitment to avoiding harmful habits. While some teammates made fun of him, he stayed true to his choices. By taking care of his body, he kept himself healthy, mentally sharp, and ready to play at the highest level. His discipline helped him compete consistently and play a key role in the Los Angeles Lakers winning three NBA championships.

Drugs and alcohol won't make you a better athlete— they do the opposite, damaging your body and clouding your judgment. These harmful habits only push us further away from God and His plan for us.

When you choose healthy habits and avoid harmful behaviors, you can play at your best and stay true to the purpose God has for you.

PUTTING IT INTO PLAY

Are your choices helping you grow as an athlete and follower of Christ? Are there any bad habits or influences that you need to stop? This week, commit to avoiding negative influences so you can be your best for God and your sport.

PRAYER

Dear Lord, thank You for the opportunities You've provided me. Please give me the strength to stay away from drugs, alcohol, and other distractions that take me away from my potential. Place people in my life who will support me and help me prioritize what truly matters. Amen.

09

OBEDIENCE IN ACTION

Remind the people to be subject to rulers and authorities, to be obedient, to be ready to do whatever is good, to slander no one, to be peaceable and considerate, and always to be gentle toward everyone.
Titus 3:1-2

LESSONS FROM THE GAME

Bad calls, unfair rulings, frustrating decisions—we've all been there. Whether it's a ref missing a foul or a coach making a decision that doesn't go your way, it's easy to let frustration take over.

But Titus 3:1-2 challenges us to respond differently: with respect, patience, and self-control.

Scottie Scheffler, one of the world's top golfers and a man known for his faith, lived this out in May 2024. On his way to the PGA Championship in Louisville, Kentucky, Scheffler got caught in heavy traffic due to a serious accident. Trying to navigate the chaos and make his tee time, he misunderstood a police officer's directions—and was suddenly arrested.

The officer, unaware of who Scheffler was, mishandled the situation. Still, instead of arguing or lashing out, Scheffler stayed calm, respectful, and obedient. He explained that he needed to reach the tournament but didn't resist arrest. Hours later, things were sorted out at the police station. Scheffler was released and able to compete, while the officer was suspended for his actions.

Scheffler later spoke about how he tried to handle the situation the right way—remaining composed and trusting that the truth would come out.

Respecting authority doesn't mean you'll always agree with decisions, but it does mean trusting that God has placed leaders in their roles for a purpose. Coaches, referees, and team captains will make mistakes, but choosing to respond with patience and integrity shows real strength.

At the same time, standing up for what's right is important, too—but it should always be done with wisdom and grace. Respecting authority doesn't mean staying silent when something is wrong; it means handling those moments with the humility and wisdom that reflect Christ.

PUTTING IT INTO PLAY

Think of a time you disagreed with a parent, teacher, or coach. Next time it happens, pause and ask God for the strength to respond respectfully and patiently, even if it feels unfair.

PRAYER

Heavenly Father, thank You for the leaders in my life.
Please give me the patience and humility to respect
and listen to them. Grant me wisdom to recognize
when to obey and when to seek help if asked to do
something against Your Word. In Jesus's name, Amen.

10

FAITH OVER FEAR

*For I know the plans I have for you," declares the
LORD, "plans to prosper you and not to harm you,
plans to give you hope and a future.*
Jeremiah 29:11

LESSONS FROM THE GAME

Bethany Hamilton's journey is one of faith, determination, and purpose. A young prodigy in the competitive surfing world, 13-year-old Hamilton was surfing off the coast of Kauai, Hawaii when a 14-foot tiger shark attacked her. The shark struck silently from below and, in an instant, took her left arm just below the shoulder. Bleeding heavily, a family friend surfing nearby saved Hamilton's life by using his shirt as a tourniquet to slow the bleeding and get her to shore.

Losing her arm seemed like the end of her dream to be a professional surfer, but it was the beginning of a story that would inspire millions. Just 26 days after the attack,

Hamilton was back on her surfboard. Two years and lots of hard work later, she won her first national surfing title, showing that faith and determination matter more than setbacks.

Jeremiah 29:11 happens to be Hamilton's favorite verse and reminds us that God's plans are bigger than our struggles. Her faith in this verse helped her do what seemed impossible. Not only did she return to surfing, but she went on to become a professional surfer. She inspired others with her faith and grit while also helping people through mentoring and charity.

Hamilton's story reveals that trusting God's path doesn't mean we won't face challenges. No one gets through life without tough times and discouragement.

But as God declares in Jeremiah 29:11, He has plans for us to prosper and succeed, not for us to fail. God won't let our struggles go to waste. Each challenge we face offers an opportunity for God to shape and prepare us to become who He wants us to be.

Like Hamilton, we can choose faith over fear, trusting that even our hardest moments shape us for something greater.

PUTTING IT INTO PLAY

What keeps you from trusting God's plan for your future? How can you lean on God's promises when life is hard? Write down Jeremiah 29:11, and let it remind you of His hope and purpose for you.

PRAYER

Dear God, thank You for the hope and future You've promised me. When I face setbacks, please help me rely on Your plan instead of my own understanding. Strengthen my faith, give me courage, and remind me that Your purpose is greater than any challenge. Amen.

11

DISCIPLINE EQUALS GROWTH

No discipline seems pleasant at the time, but painful. Later on, however, it produces a harvest of righteousness and peace for those who have been trained by it.

Hebrews 12:11

LESSONS FROM THE GAME

Great athletes aren't just built on talent—they're built on discipline.

We can't always rely on our feelings and motivation to push us through the grind of practice or training. If we do, we risk getting distracted, procrastinating, or giving up altogether.

No one understands this better than former Alabama football coach Nick Saban. Over 17 years at the University of Alabama, Saban produced 133 NFL draft picks and won six national championships. He turned countless high school athletes into NFL superstars. His secret? Making discipline a non-negotiable part of his players' mindset.

As Saban says, "The bridge that we all have to cross is feeling vs. choice." For him, self-discipline comes down to two key decisions:

1. "There's something I know I'm supposed to do that I really don't want to do. Can you make yourself do it?"

2. "There's something you know you're not supposed to do, but you want to do it. Can you keep yourself from it?"

The same goes for spiritual discipline. With school, sports, and everything else competing for our attention, it's easy to let spiritual habits slip. But just as strength training builds physical muscle, consistent time in prayer and Scripture builds our spiritual muscles. Even a few minutes each day in God's Word strengthens our faith, grounds us, and brings peace—just like a daily workout keeps an athlete in shape.

Discipline isn't always easy, but the rewards make it worth it in the long run. The habits you build today will shape who you become.

Hebrews 12:11 assures us that if we stay disciplined, we'll see the rewards of peace and growth, even if it doesn't feel like it at the moment.

PUTTING IT INTO PLAY

Where in your life could you use more discipline? Pick one small habit and stick with it. Over time, that discipline will compound into real growth.

PRAYER

Dear God, please guide me to remain disciplined in my faith, sports, and studies. Support me as I work hard and face challenges in the areas of my life where I want to grow. Remind me of the value of discipline, especially when I'm tempted to give in to complacency or laziness. Amen.

12

FUELING YOUR PURPOSE

Do you not know that your bodies are temples of the Holy Spirit, who is in you, whom you have received from God? You are not your own; you were bought at a price. Therefore honor God with your bodies.
1 Corinthians 6:19-20

LESSONS FROM THE GAME

Every athlete looks for an edge—better training, better gear, better coaching. But one of the biggest performance factors is something simple: what you put into your body.

At the 2008 Beijing Olympics, top U.S. swimmer Ryan Lochte had a diet far from what you'd expect of a world-class athlete. For two weeks, Lochte ate almost nothing but fast food from McDonald's. For years, his coaches asked him to clean up his eating habits, warning that his poor diet was holding him back. Lochte's wake-up call came during a series of fitness tests, which showed a lot of room for improvement if he ate healthier.

Motivated by the test results, Lochte improved his diet to prepare for the 2012 London Olympics. The change paid off. He improved in the pool and went on to win five medals. Lochte's story proves that what you put into your body affects how you perform.

But have you ever considered what you feed your mind?

Just like junk food holds us back from peak physical performance, consuming content that doesn't align with God's standards can negatively impact our thoughts and spiritual well-being. The Bible encourages us to guard our hearts and minds because everything we do flows from them.

What you feed your body fuels your performance—what you feed your mind fuels your faith. Make sure both honor God.

PUTTING IT INTO PLAY

Consider the shows, music, and online content you consume. Does it honor God? Today, choose uplifting content that strengthens your mind and spirit. Set boundaries for your online activity to make sure it's building you up and not tearing you down.

PRAYER

Dear Lord, thank You for the gift of my body and
the ability to choose what I consume. Please help
me stay mindful of what I allow into my body and
mind, seeking only those things that honor You. May
my choices nourish both my body and my spirit. In
Jesus's name, Amen.

13

TEAMWORK IN MOTION

Two are better than one, because they have a good return for their
labor: If either of them falls down, one can help the other up.
But pity anyone who falls and has no one to help them up.
Ecclesiastes 4:9-10

LESSONS FROM THE GAME

No athlete succeeds alone.

Even in individual sports, success comes from the people behind the scenes—coaches, trainers, teammates, and family—who help push you forward. The best athletes don't just rely on themselves; they lean on the people around them.

A powerful example of teamwork is the Tour de France, a grueling 23-day cycling race where victory depends on more than individual skill. Success in this race is built on the collective effort of a team, as demonstrated by cycling champion Chris Froome and his four Tour de France wins.

Each Tour, Froome's teammates worked tirelessly to position him for the win. They took turns riding in front to shield him from the wind, helping him conserve energy. This strategy provided Froome the strength to surge ahead at key moments and distance himself from the competition. His teammates sacrificed their own rankings to ensure his success—without them, his victories wouldn't have been possible.

We all know that individual effort matters, but it's the support from others that helps us hit those bigger goals. Teamwork isn't just a sports strategy—it's how God designed us to live. Froome's success shows us the wisdom in Ecclesiastes 4:9-10, which teaches us that we're stronger when we help each other.

Just as Froome had teammates helping push him forward, we need people who challenge, support, and encourage us in our faith journey. The Christian life isn't meant to be a solo race. We grow stronger when we walk alongside others—celebrating victories, tackling struggles, and keeping each other focused on God.

PUTTING IT INTO PLAY

Think about the "team" God has placed in your life. It could be your family, sports team, church, or community. How can you step up to support them or lighten their load?

PRAYER

Dear Lord, thank You for the community You've
placed in my life. Please help me appreciate the power
of teamwork, encourage those around me, and be
a friend who lifts others up. Teach me to work with
unity, kindness, and purpose so we can honor You
together. Amen.

14

PATIENCE IS KEY

Be still before the LORD and wait patiently for him; do not fret when people succeed in their ways, when they carry out their wicked schemes.

Psalm 37:7

LESSONS FROM THE GAME

Kurt Warner's journey to NFL stardom wasn't easy—it was a test of patience and faith.

Warner wasn't supposed to make it to the NFL. He wasn't a five-star recruit and didn't play for a powerhouse college football program. By the time he graduated from the University of Northern Iowa, no NFL team wanted him. With no offers, he stocked grocery store shelves to make ends meet while playing in the Arena Football League. Warner refused to give up on his NFL dreams.

Many athletes in Warner's position would have quit or chosen an easier path. But Psalm 37:7 instructs us to "be still before the LORD and wait patiently for him." Warner did just that. He continued to put in the effort and trusted that God had a plan, even when things didn't go as expected.

Warner's perseverance paid off when he got a chance with the St. Louis Rams, leading to one of the greatest success stories in NFL history. He helped the Rams win the 1999 Super Bowl and was named both league and Super Bowl MVP. His success didn't end there. Warner went on to have a remarkable career and eventually earned a spot in the Pro Football Hall of Fame.

Whether you're waiting for your big moment or struggling through setbacks, trust that God's timing is always perfect. If Warner had given up during his toughest years, he would have missed out on the amazing things God had in store for him. Don't let impatience keep you from what God is preparing you for.

PUTTING IT INTO PLAY

Think about an area in your life where you feel impatient about your progress. Maybe your strength in the weight room isn't increasing as quickly as you'd like, or your times aren't improving as fast as you want them to. How can you change your mindset to trust God's plan and keep working hard?

PRAYER

Dear God, thank You for Kurt Warner's example of patience and perseverance. Please help me trust in Your perfect timing and remain faithful as I wait. Teach me to be patient in the process, knowing that each challenge is an opportunity to grow and prepare for the future You have in store for me. Amen.

15

SELFLESS IN SPIRIT

Do nothing out of selfish ambition or vain conceit. Rather, in humility value others above yourselves, not looking to your own interests but each of you to the interests of the others.
Philippians 2:3-4

LESSONS FROM THE GAME

Many athletes dream of standing on the Olympic podium. Lawrence Lemieux had that chance—until he gave it up to save someone else.

In the 1988 Seoul Olympics, the Canadian sailor was in second place, well on his way to a medal in the Finn class race. But as he sailed through the rough waters, he noticed a capsized boat from another event. Two sailors had been thrown overboard and were struggling in the waves.

Without hesitation, Lemieux abandoned his race and turned toward the stranded sailors. By the time he rejoined, he had dropped to 22nd place—his shot at

Olympic glory was gone. Although he lost his chance at a medal, his selfless act was an amazing example of what Philippians 2:3-4 teaches us about putting the needs of others before ourselves.

In sports, our drive to compete can sometimes overshadow everything, making it easy to focus only on personal success. But as Lemieux's story shows, true greatness isn't just about winning—it's about knowing when to put others first.

The same is true in life. Whether in school, work, friendships, or family, God calls us to live humbly and selflessly, just like Jesus did. Jesus gave up everything for us, and we can strive to follow His example by being humble and helping others, even when it's hard or costs us something.

PUTTING IT INTO PLAY

This week, find a way to help someone else. It could be as simple as helping a teammate with homework or giving them a ride home. Remember, true greatness isn't just about coming in first—it's about lifting others up along the way.

PRAYER

Dear Jesus, thank You for being the perfect example of unselfishness and sacrifice. Please help me think of others and be willing to help, even when it means giving up something important. Fill my heart with compassion and guide me to show kindness in all that I do. Amen.

16

JESUS WON

I have told you these things, so that in me you may have peace. In this world you will have trouble. But take heart! I have overcome the world.

John 16:33

LESSONS FROM THE GAME

Most MLB rookies try to keep their heads down in their first season—blending in, earning respect, and proving they belong. But when Evan Carter arrived at spring training with the Texas Rangers in 2023, he made a different kind of statement. During warm-ups, he boldly wore a T-shirt that read, "Jesus Won."

For Carter, this was more than a slogan—it was a reminder. His identity wasn't tied to stats or performance but to Jesus's triumph over life's struggles.

That same message resonates with athletes like C.J. Fite, a defensive lineman at Arizona State University.

Along with several of his teammates, Fite proudly wears the *Jesus Won* shirt as a public declaration of his faith. As Fite put it, "Just to start, He won the grave." To Fite, *Jesus Won* isn't just a phrase—it's a foundation.

At Ohio State University, over 20 football players took this message even further, wearing *Jesus Won* shirts during their 2024 training camp. In the high-pressure world of college football, boldly expressing faith can be intimidating. But these athletes didn't hesitate. Together, they stood firm in their belief, carrying that same confidence throughout the season—all the way to a national championship.

The *Jesus Won* message has spread far beyond a T-shirt. It's a statement of faith, a source of peace, and a reminder that no matter what happens on the field or in life, the victory has already been won. As Jesus tells us in John 16:33, life will bring challenges—but we can move forward with confidence, knowing He has already overcome them all.

PUTTING IT INTO PLAY

If you face a tough practice, a big test, or a conflict this week, remember—you don't need a T-shirt to know that *Jesus Won*. Let His victory over sin and death give you strength and remind you of what truly matters.

PRAYER

Dear Jesus, thank You for granting me the ultimate victory through Your death on the cross so I don't have to face life's challenges alone. Help me rely on Your strength when things get hard and remember Your greater plan. Let my words and actions reflect my trust and hope in You. Amen.

17

YOUR HARVEST IS COMING

Let us not become weary in doing good, for at the proper time we will reap a harvest if we do not give up.
Galatians 6:9

LESSONS FROM THE GAME

You put in the hours—early mornings, long practices, late-night homework—but sometimes, it can feel like nothing is paying off. Maybe your shot isn't landing, your swing isn't improving, or no one notices your effort. It can be frustrating, but remember, progress takes time.

Galatians 6:9 teaches us that God rewards persistence in His timing. Even when results feel distant, every step forward matters.

Few athletes understand this better than Paralympian Noelle Lambert. A standout Division 1 lacrosse player at UMass Lowell, she had no idea her biggest challenge would come far from the field. One day, while riding her moped, she collided with a dump truck, severing her leg on impact. A bystander acted quickly, using his shirt as a tourniquet to slow the bleeding, saving her life.

When she woke up in the hospital, Lambert had a choice—dwell on what she had lost or focus on what she could still achieve. She decided to concentrate on what she could control: her hard work and determination.

Though progress was slow, Lambert kept at it, making an incredible recovery and becoming the first above-the-knee amputee to play Division 1 college lacrosse.

After graduating, she set her sights on a new goal: competing in the Paralympic Games. Since lacrosse wasn't part of the Paralympics, she shifted her attention to sprinting. Lambert's dedication led her to the Tokyo 2021 Paralympic Games, where she finished 6th in the 100-meter sprint and broke the American record.

Your "harvest" might not be a trophy but could be a stronger faith, greater resilience, or new opportunities. Trust God's timing, keep showing up, and don't stop now—what you're working toward may be closer than you think.

PUTTING IT INTO PLAY

Next time you face a challenge or injury, focus on making progress, even if it's a little at a time. Celebrate your small wins and pray for patience. Trust that growth is happening, even if you can't see it yet.

PRAYER

Heavenly Father, thank You for showing me that my hard work is never wasted. Please help me trust that my effort and persistence are drawing me closer to a breakthrough in growth. When I face setbacks, remind me that You are working in the background, preparing something great for me. Amen.

18

STRENGTH IN GRATITUDE

Give thanks in all circumstances; for this is God's will
for you in Christ Jesus.
1 Thessalonians 5:18

LESSONS FROM THE GAME

When everything's going right, and you're performing at your best, it's easy to feel grateful for the blessings in your life. But what about when things go wrong?

1 Thessalonians 5:18 tells us to give thanks in all situations, not just the good ones. But let's face it, that's easier said than done. No one naturally feels thankful after a tough loss, a bad injury, or a frustrating setback.

But gratitude isn't about ignoring your emotions—it's okay to feel disappointed or upset.

Gratitude helps us gain perspective, reminding us that even when things aren't perfect, we still have plenty of blessings to be thankful for.

Few athletes have lived this out like Dak Prescott. In 2020, the Dallas Cowboys quarterback suffered a devastating ankle injury against the New York Giants, ending his season instantly. But instead of dwelling on his setback, Prescott chose gratitude and focused on his faith.

During his recovery, he confidently stated: "I'm just excited—excited for God's purpose and plan. I know it's bigger than anything that I see or I could have imagined, but I'm trusting Him… all this will be a great comeback and a great story," Prescott said.

True to his words, he came back stronger than ever. In the 2021 season, he set a franchise record with 37 touchdown passes, leading the Cowboys to become the league's top offense.

Prescott's response wasn't about pretending everything was fine but about trusting that God was still working. Gratitude isn't just for the good times; it's a mindset that keeps us grounded in faith, no matter the situation.

PUTTING IT INTO PLAY

Think of a recent challenge—can you identify one thing to be thankful for, like a friend's support or a moment of laughter? Start writing these down daily, and over time, you'll be amazed at how much you really have to be thankful for.

PRAYER

Dear Lord, thank You for always being by my side. When things don't go my way, help me trust Your plan and choose gratitude. Please open my eyes to see how You're working in my life. Amen.

19

FROM DEFEAT TO VICTORY

Therefore, if anyone is in Christ, the new creation has come:
The old has gone, the new is here!
2 Corinthians 5:17

LESSONS FROM THE GAME

A #1 seed had never lost to a #16 seed in NCAA basketball tournament history—until the University of Virginia did.

In March 2018, the Virginia Cavaliers entered March Madness as one of the best college teams in the country, seen as strong contenders for the national title. But in a stunning first-round upset, they were knocked out by the University of Maryland, Baltimore County (UMBC)— the lowest-seeded team in the tournament. A team that had dominated all season suddenly found itself on the wrong side of history.

But instead of letting that defeat define them, the Cavaliers used it to fuel their motivation. In 2019, they stormed back to the tournament with a renewed sense of purpose. They battled their way to the championship game, facing the Texas Tech Red Raiders in what became an instant classic. After a hard-fought overtime, the Cavaliers won their first-ever national title.

The Cavaliers had turned the biggest upset in March Madness history into one of the greatest basketball comebacks ever—all in just one year. Their victory proves that failure isn't the end; it can ignite the path to redemption.

As 2 Corinthians 5:17 tells us, we are made new through Jesus, who conquered sin and saved us through His death on the cross. When we choose to follow Him, He offers us a fresh start. Our past mistakes, sins, and shortcomings no longer have to define us.

The Virginia Cavaliers didn't let their disappointing end to the 2017-18 season limit their future, and we don't have to let our past failures hold us back either.

PUTTING IT INTO PLAY

Is there a mistake or failure from your past that you're still holding onto? Remember that God's grace can help you let it go. With God's help, you can leave the past behind and live as the new person He has made you to be.

From Defeat to Victory

PRAYER

Dear Lord, please forgive my past sins and mistakes. Thank You for the new life and salvation I have through Your Son, Jesus. May my past shape me but not define me. Help me overcome my struggles and live in the victory You've already won for me. Amen.

20

THE HEART OF LEADERSHIP

Don't let anyone look down on you because you are young, but set
an example for the believers in speech, in conduct,
in love, in faith and in purity.
1 Timothy 4:12

LESSONS FROM THE GAME

Some athletes lead with their voice. Others lead by example. The best do both.

Leadership isn't about being the loudest or the most experienced—it's about how you carry yourself and impact those around you.

That's why 1 Timothy 4:12 reminds us that being young doesn't disqualify you from leadership. In this verse, Paul encouraged a young Timothy to set an example through his actions, proving that real influence comes from character, not age. CJ Stroud, quarterback for the Houston Texans, is proving that same truth.

At just 22 years old, Stroud led the Texans to the 2023 NFL Playoffs with tremendous poise and skill. In a dominant win over the Cleveland Browns, he became the youngest quarterback in NFL history to secure a playoff victory, showing that leadership isn't about age—it's about stepping up when it matters most.

And Stroud's leadership goes beyond the game. He boldly shares his Christian faith, often saying that football is more than just a sport—it's a platform God has given him to spread the Gospel and encourage others in their walk with Christ. His confidence in using his influence for something greater than himself shows that leadership isn't just about titles, but about purpose.

In Matthew 5:16, Jesus encourages us to let our light shine so others can see God through us. Every practice, game, and conversation is a chance to lead—not just with skill, but with integrity and faith. When we strive for excellence and serve others with humility, we don't just influence—we reflect Christ in everything we do.

PUTTING IT INTO PLAY

How can you set a good example this week? Whether it's a cheerful attitude, putting in extra effort at practice, or mentoring another teammate, look for ways to uplift those around you.

PRAYER

Dear God, thank You for the opportunity to influence others positively. Please help me set an example through my attitude, work ethic, and relationships. May my actions reflect Jesus's love and leave a lasting impact on my teammates and friends. Amen.

21

THROUGH THICK AND THIN

*A friend loves at all times, and a brother is born
for a time of adversity.*
Proverbs 17:17

LESSONS FROM THE GAME

True teamwork isn't tested when things are going right—it's revealed when everything's going wrong.

What happens when a teammate makes a mistake that costs the game? The real test of friendship and loyalty comes when blaming someone is easier than standing by their side.

In the 2019 MLB playoffs, Clayton Kershaw, a top pitcher for the Los Angeles Dodgers, faced a heartbreaking moment in Game 5 of the National League Division Series against the Washington Nationals. With the stakes high in this elimination game, Kershaw gave up back-to-back home runs in the 8th inning.

Those two mistakes changed the game, and the Dodgers ended up losing. With everything on the line, Kershaw likely thought the blame was his to carry.

But instead of blaming him, Kershaw's teammates stood by him. Players like Max Muncy and Kenley Jansen quickly came to his defense publicly, reminding everyone that Kershaw had been one of the team's best players all season. Instead of tearing Kershaw down, they had his back.

This is exactly what Proverbs 17:17 instructs us to do. True friends and teammates are there for you in life's challenging moments, not just the easy ones. Kershaw's teammates embodied true friendship and loyalty by standing with him during a difficult time. They did so out of genuine care and commitment, not obligation.

A real teammate supports you in your struggles, even when it doesn't benefit them.

PUTTING IT INTO PLAY

When things go wrong, are you the kind of friend or teammate who sticks around, or do you walk away? Do the people around you know they can count on you when it matters most? Think about one person who might need your support right now. Send them a quick message, check-in, or say something encouraging to show you care.

PRAYER

Dear God, thank You for the friends You've placed in my life. Help me stand by them in tough times, just as I want them to do for me. Please give me the compassion to show up, support them, and stay loyal, even when inconvenient. Amen.

22

CALM OVER CONFLICT

You have heard that it was said, 'Eye for eye, and tooth for tooth.'
But I tell you, do not resist an evil person. If anyone slaps you on
the right cheek, turn to them the other cheek also.
Matthew 5:38-39

LESSONS FROM THE GAME

Competition can get heated, especially when taunts and cheap shots come into play. It's tempting to clap back when we're insulted or pushed to our limits. But in Matthew 5:38-39, Jesus teaches us to respond with self-control and grace rather than retaliation.

In the 2006 FIFA World Cup final, the match between France and Italy was tied 1-1 and locked in extra time. Zinedine Zidane, a French midfielder and one of the world's best players was competing in the final match of his career. In the last few minutes of extra time, an Italian player insulted Zidane's sister to provoke him. In response, Zidane headbutted him in the chest, knocking him flat to the ground. Zidane was immediately given a red card and ejected from the game.

With Zidane out of the game and France playing without their captain, the team became disjointed, lost momentum, and ultimately fell to Italy in a penalty shootout.

Zidane's impulsive response offers us an important lesson about how to react when provoked. It's natural to get upset when others insult us, but our reactions matter. Instead of letting our emotions get the best of us, we can choose to respond with self-control.

Paul reminds us in Romans 12:19, "Do not take revenge, my dear friends, but leave room for God's wrath, for it is written: 'It is mine to avenge; I will repay,' says the Lord."

"Turning the other cheek" doesn't make you weak—it takes real strength. Trusting God's justice frees us from the burden of revenge and allows Him to handle things in His perfect timing. This doesn't mean we should stay in harm's way—it means trusting God to lead our response.

PUTTING IT INTO PLAY

Next time someone tries to provoke or upset you, stop and choose a response that honors God. Instead of seeking revenge, offer silence, a calm response, or walk away. Think about how Jesus stayed calm and showed love, even when insulted. Let His example guide you.

PRAYER

Dear Jesus, thank You for Your example of self-control and grace. Please help me resist the urge to react in anger when provoked. Remind me that justice is best served by Your hands, not mine. Amen.

23

FULLY COMMITTED

I know your deeds, that you are neither cold nor hot. I wish you were either one or the other! So, because you are lukewarm— neither hot nor cold—I am about to spit you out of my mouth.
Revelation 3:15-16

LESSONS FROM THE GAME

Imagine a coach telling you, "I wish you'd either play full speed or just sit on the bench." In the same way, God invites us to grow in our faith—not to be perfect, but to be intentional in pursuing our relationship with Him.

This kind of all-in mindset is what separates good athletes from great ones. No one knew this better than NBA Hall of Famer Kobe Bryant. His legendary work ethic wasn't about being the best overnight—it was about showing up every day, putting in the work, and refusing to settle for anything less than his best effort.

Determined to gain an edge over his competition, Bryant often worked out six hours a day, arriving at the gym before sunrise and staying long after others had left. He never stopped perfecting his game, whether practicing game situations or fine-tuning his jump shot. His famous quote summed up his mindset: "Rest in the end, not in the middle."

That kind of commitment isn't just for sports. In Revelation 3:15-16, God warns against being "lukewarm" in our faith. He doesn't want half-hearted devotion—He calls us to be all in.

Bryant's success wasn't accidental. Without his relentless training and drive to improve, he wouldn't have become one of the greatest players of all time.

Faith works the same way. Growing spiritually requires effort and consistency.

While trophies and titles are the reward in sports, life offers something far greater: eternal joy in Heaven. One day, your life will be viewed like a highlight reel. Will your faith stand out?

PUTTING IT INTO PLAY

Are you committed to living out your faith? Or are you just going through the motions? This week, choose to be more "all in" for God. Maybe this looks like joining a youth group or seeking mentorship from a fellow believer.

PRAYER

Heavenly Father, I want to be all in with my faith.
Please help me look past my selfish desires and keep
my eyes on eternity. Amen.

24

PLAYING BY THE RULES

Similarly, anyone who competes as an athlete does not receive the victor's crown except by competing according to the rules.
2 Timothy 2:5

LESSONS FROM THE GAME

In sports, the rules aren't there just to keep things honest and safe.

They set boundaries that protect the integrity of the competition and ensure everyone has a fair shot at victory.

When an athlete steps outside those boundaries—intentionally or not—it has consequences. Just ask Anna Cockrell, who experienced this firsthand at the 2021 Tokyo Olympics. The American hurdler was disqualified from the women's 400-meter hurdles after breaking a technical rule when her foot crossed into a neighboring lane on the track. Although it seemed like a minor slip-up, it cost her a chance to compete in the finals, where she had a strong shot at winning a medal.

Just as Cockrell lost her chance to advance when she went off course, we risk missing out on the incredible life God has planned for us when we stray from His path.

While rules are meant to guard the integrity of competition, God's rules are designed to guard the integrity of our hearts. God's Word is our guide to living a life that honors Him and leads to peace and, ultimately, eternal life in Heaven. And though we all make mistakes as part of being human, those mistakes don't have to define us. God's forgiveness offers us the chance to start over with a clean slate.

Cockrell didn't let her mistake define her. After learning a tough lesson from her 2021 disqualification, she trained harder and came back to win silver at the 2024 Olympics. Her story connects to 2 Timothy 2:5—an athlete has to follow the rules to win. But in faith, the "victor's crown" isn't a trophy or medal—it's the gift of salvation, given to those who follow Jesus.

Just like you can't win in sports by ignoring the rules, you can't receive God's ultimate reward by going your own way. God calls us to follow Him—trusting in Jesus, turning away from sin, and living out His Word.

PUTTING IT INTO PLAY

Think about a part of your life where you might be tempted to ignore God's instructions or take the easy way out. Ask God for the strength to stay on track. Remember that His guidance will lead you to a better life.

PRAYER

Dear Lord, thank You for showing me that true victory comes from following Your Word. Please help me stay faithful, even when shortcuts seem easier. Guide me to live in a way that honors You. Amen.

25

VICTORY THROUGH SACRIFICE

*Carry each other's burdens, and in this way you will
fulfill the law of Christ.*
Galatians 6:2

LESSONS FROM THE GAME

The scorching heat of the 2016 ITU World Triath-
lon Series Final in Mexico pushed every competitor
to their limit. Among them were brothers Alistair and
Jonny Brownlee, elite triathletes representing the United
Kingdom.

Despite the harsh race conditions, Jonny pushed himself to the front of the pack, leading the race with just
around 400 meters to go. His victory seemed inevitable
until the heat began to take its toll. Jonny started to stum-
ble, losing control of his legs as his body threatened to
give out completely.

From behind, Alistair noticed his brother was in trouble. Alistair was locked in a tight race for second place with South Africa's Henri Schoeman. But with Jonny slowing and about to lose the lead, the gold medal would now go to either Alistair or Schoeman.

Instead of chasing his own victory, Alistair ran to his brother's side. He placed Jonny's arm over his shoulders and supported him to the finish line. Meanwhile, Schoeman surged ahead and claimed first place.

When asked later why he gave up his chance to win, Alistair humbly indicated he would never leave his brother behind when he needed help.

By sacrificing his chance to win by helping Jonny, Alistair demonstrated what it means to carry someone's burden. Alistair's choice highlights the truth of Galatians 6:2: carrying someone's burden—especially when it costs us something—is a powerful way to show God's love.

Helping others through their struggles not only shows basic kindness but also spreads the selfless love of Jesus. Even though our sacrifices may be small compared to the one Jesus made for us, they can still point others to Him.

PUTTING IT INTO PLAY

What's one small thing you can do today to make someone's load a little lighter? Maybe it's sticking around after practice to help clean up or sending a quick text to check on a friend.

PRAYER

Dear God, thank You for the ultimate sacrifice of Your one and only Son, who gave His life for our benefit. Please help me understand the true meaning of sacrifice and the joy in giving something up for the good of others. Guide me to serve others with a willing and selfless heart. Amen.

26

YOUR TALENTS, HIS GLORY

We have different gifts, according to the grace given to each of us. If your gift is prophesying, then prophesy in accordance with your faith.
Romans 12:6

LESSONS FROM THE GAME

Everyone has unique talents. Maybe yours is crushing a fastball, delivering a powerful volleyball spike, or throwing a perfect spiral. But Romans 12:6 reminds us that our gifts aren't just for personal success—they're meant to honor God.

Sydney McLaughlin-Levrone, the American Olympian and world record-holder in track and field, is celebrated for her exceptional skills in hurdling and sprinting. At just 16 years old, she became the youngest U.S. track and field athlete to compete in the Olympics in nearly 40 years. After winning the 400-meter hurdles at the 2024 Paris Olympics, she became the first woman ever to win back-to-back gold medals in the event.

In a post-race interview, she attributed all her success to God, saying, "I credit all that I do to God. He's given me a gift. He's given me a drive. ... I have a platform, and I want to use it to glorify Him." McLaughlin knows that God didn't give her talents for personal glory alone. She understands that she is called to use the platform her skills have provided to honor God and leave a positive impact on those around her.

God uses our individuality and unique skill sets to show that we are all valuable and have a role in carrying out His will. With this in mind, we should be thoughtful about what we use our gifts to accomplish.

When we use our abilities to serve others and reflect God's goodness, we turn our talents into something greater than personal achievement. Every skill, opportunity, and success is a chance to point back to Him and show gratitude for the talents He's trusted us with.

PUTTING IT INTO PLAY

Look for ways to use your talents to help others this week. Maybe there's a teammate who could use your guidance or a classmate you could help study for a tough exam. Challenge yourself to use your abilities to serve others, spread God's love, and bring glory to His name.

PRAYER

Dear God, thank You for the unique gifts You've given me. Help me use them not for my glory but to serve others and share Your love. Please guide me to use my abilities to make a lasting impact on Your Kingdom. Amen.

27

OWN THE OUTCOME

So then, each of us will give an account of ourselves to God.
Romans 14:12

LESSONS FROM THE GAME

In the 2023 NFL Playoffs, the Buffalo Bills met the Kansas City Chiefs in a high-stakes Divisional Round matchup. With just over seven minutes left in the fourth quarter and the Bills trailing 24-27, quarterback Josh Allen took control of the game. He led his team on a hard-fought 15-play drive, pushing them into field goal range. Allen had done his part, putting the Bills in position to tie the game and force overtime.

Now, everything rested on kicker Tyler Bass. A 44-yard field goal stood between the Bills and a chance to extend their playoff hopes. With the game on the line, Bass missed the kick, sending the ball wide right. The Bills' season came to a heartbreaking end, while the Chiefs advanced to the AFC Championship and went on to win the Super Bowl.

While Bass's missed kick was the final play, many moments throughout a game shape any win or loss. Still, Bass took full responsibility for the defeat, saying, "Ultimately, it's completely on me. I've got to do a better job of getting through to my target." Instead of pointing fingers at where his teammates had fallen short, he owned the moment—demonstrating humility and accountability in the face of intense pressure.

Much like Bass took full responsibility for his role in the game, we are called to take ownership of our actions, especially in our relationship with God. Romans 14:12 reminds us that, in the end, we will each give an account of ourselves to God. Our choices (good and bad) are ours alone, and we can't shift responsibility onto others. Just as Bass didn't blame his teammates, we are responsible for how we live regardless of what anyone else does.

PUTTING IT INTO PLAY

Think about a time when you made a mistake or faced a difficult situation. Did you take responsibility, or did you blame someone or something else? This week, find one part of your life—your actions, words, or attitude— where you can take full responsibility.

PRAYER

Heavenly Father, thank You for Your grace
and forgiveness. Please embolden my heart to
take responsibility for my actions and decisions.
Strengthen my character so that my choices align with
Your teachings and uphold Your will. Amen.

28

ONE BODY, ONE MISSION

Just as a body, though one, has many parts, but all its many parts form one body, so it is with Christ. For we were all baptized by one Spirit so as to form one body—whether Jews or Gentiles, slave or free—and we were all given the one Spirit to drink. Even so the body is not made up of one part but of many.
1 Corinthians 12:12-14

LESSONS FROM THE GAME

The 2022 World Cup Final wasn't just a showdown between Argentina and France—it was a masterclass in teamwork.

Argentina's victory wasn't about one standout player. Their win was a team effort, with each player stepping up to use their special talents.

Lionel Messi delivered two crucial goals, including a clutch extra-time shot. Emiliano Martínez made a game-saving block in the final seconds of extra time and helped seal the win in the penalty shootout. Cristian Romero held down the defense, cutting off France's attacks. Every role was different, but every contribution mattered.

That's exactly how God designed us to function. In 1 Corinthians 12:12-14, Paul compares the body of Christ to a human body—many parts, each with a purpose, working together as one.

Think about it: A soccer team needs scorers, defenders, and goalkeepers. A track team isn't just about sprinters—distance runners, hurdlers, throwers, and jumpers each contribute points that lead to a team win. The body of Christ is no different—some lead, some encourage, some step up when others need support. No role is too small.

Striving for personal excellence is important, but the real impact comes when you see how your gifts fit into something bigger—and embrace the role God has for you.

PUTTING IT INTO PLAY

What unique gifts has God given you? Are you gifted in encouraging, leading, teaching, or bringing people together? How can you use your gifts to bless someone else? No matter how small, every contribution is valuable when we work together.

One Body, One Mission

PRAYER

Dear Lord, thank You for making me a part of Your body and giving me a special role in Your plan. Please help me appreciate the gifts You've given me and use them to work together with others so I can advance Your Kingdom. Amen.

29

THE POWER OF THE UNDERDOG

But God chose the foolish things of the world to shame the wise;
God chose the weak things of the world to shame the strong.
1 Corinthians 1:27

LESSONS FROM THE GAME

The world watched in disbelief as a group of young American hockey players took down the most dominant team in the sport. In the 1980 Winter Olympics, the U.S. team pulled off one of the greatest upsets in history, defeating the nearly unbeatable Soviet Union team.

The Soviets were seasoned champions. They had won four straight Olympic gold medals and dominated international hockey for two decades. On the other hand, the U.S. team consisted of college players—not professionals—who had never competed at such an elite level.

When the two teams faced off in the Olympic medal round, the Soviets took an early lead. The U.S. fought back, tying the game twice before scoring the go-ahead goal in the third period. With just seconds left, they held on to secure the unforgettable "Miracle on Ice."

Being the underdog can feel overwhelming. Perhaps your team is facing a stronger, more experienced opponent. Or maybe you feel outmatched by others with more skill. But as the U.S. Olympic hockey team proved, heart, effort, and belief can defy all odds.

1 Corinthians 1:27 shows that God can use what seems weak to accomplish incredible things. God doesn't need you to be the strongest or most talented. He looks for hearts willing to trust Him and give their best. Like David, who defeated Goliath with only faith and a slingshot, you can overcome challenges beyond your strength when you trust God to equip you.

When you're the underdog, remember that God can turn things around. He loves to work through people who seem overlooked or outmatched, showing that victory comes from Him. Even if the scoreboard doesn't reflect it, playing with courage, faith, and effort is always a win in God's eyes.

PUTTING IT INTO PLAY

Next time you face a team that seems unbeatable, focus on playing with faith, heart, and fundamentals rather than worrying about the odds. Ask God to work through your team's courage and effort, and trust Him with the outcome.

PRAYER

Dear God, thank You for showing me victory isn't about being the strongest or most skilled but about trusting You with big challenges. Please help me play with faith and confidence in You. May my efforts reflect Your strength and bring You honor, no matter the odds. Amen.

30

GAME DAY

*Commit to the LORD whatever you do,
and he will establish your plans.*
Proverbs 16:3

LESSONS FROM THE GAME

You prepare your body before a game—stretching, visualizing success, and listening to your favorite songs. But do you prepare your heart the same way?

Pre-game routines help us get in the zone, building confidence and focus before the competition begins. They calm our nerves and set us up to perform at our best. Just as warming up prepares our bodies for peak performance, spiritual preparation helps our hearts and minds do the same.

Before the game, set aside time to pray. Thank God for the opportunity to compete, and ask Him to help you play with heart and discipline. Surrender your performance to Him, trusting He will use it for His purpose—win or lose.

As you pray, go beyond just asking for success. Pray for your teammates to play with unity, your coaches to have wisdom, and everyone's safety on the field. If nerves creep in, remind yourself that God is with you every moment, giving you strength and peace.

Once the game starts, strive to honor Christ in how you play—through your effort, your attitude, and how you treat your teammates, coaches, opponents, and officials. You won't always do it perfectly, but aiming to compete in a way that honors Christ will set you apart.

When you compete with a heart devoted to God, you'll find peace, even in high-pressure moments. No matter the outcome, you'll walk away knowing you gave your best, played with integrity, and honored Him through your actions.

PUTTING IT INTO PLAY

Do you set aside time to connect with God before you compete? Before your next game, take a moment to pray, alone or with teammates. Talk with God about what's on your mind and commit your efforts to Him.

PRAYER

Dear Lord, thank You for the opportunity to compete and the talents You've given me. Help me focus my heart and mind on You. Please grant me the strength, perseverance, and clarity to play my best. May my attitude, effort, and sportsmanship honor You, no matter the result. Amen.

31

FOLLOW THE GAME PLAN

Do not merely listen to the word, and so deceive yourselves.
Do what it says.
James 1:22

LESSONS FROM THE GAME

At the 2006 Winter Olympics, American Lindsey Jacobellis was moments away from Olympic gold. She had dominated the Snowboard Cross final, navigating the obstacles of the snow-covered course with ease. With only two jumps remaining and a huge lead, all she had to do was ride clean and finish strong.

But at the last moment, Jacobellis decided to add a flashy move, one that wasn't necessary. While trying to show off, she lost her balance and fell. As she scrambled to recover, Switzerland's Tanja Frieden flew past her, snatching the gold medal and leaving Jacobellis with the silver.

Jacobellis didn't lack skill—she failed to follow her game plan. She knew all she needed to do was finish smoothly, but in the heat of the moment, she strayed from the plan.

We can compare this to what James 1:22 cautions us about. It's not enough to know the right thing to do. We must actually do it. We can read, hear, and recite God's Word, but we're missing the point if we don't put it into practice.

Following God's teachings doesn't guarantee us a struggle-free life, but His Word provides us wisdom to navigate the challenges we'll face.

When we live according to His Word, we open ourselves to experiencing true peace, purpose, and direction. The Bible is a blueprint for making wiser choices, building stronger relationships, and living a fulfilling life. The more we follow its instructions, the more we'll see our lives transformed for the better.

PUTTING IT INTO PLAY

Is there a situation where you know the right thing to do but haven't followed through? What's been holding you back from taking that step? Today, choose one step that brings you closer to doing what you know is right.

PRAYER

Dear Jesus, thank You for Your guidance. Please help me not only hear Your Word but also live it out daily. Grant me the strength to follow through on what You've called me to do, even when it's not easy. Amen.

32

TRUSTING GOD IN THE FIRE

In their hearts humans plan their course, but the LORD establishes their steps.
Proverbs 16:9

LESSONS FROM THE GAME

In 2017, Philadelphia Eagles quarterback Carson Wentz was living every NFL player's dream—until everything changed in an instant.

At just 24 years old, Wentz was leading the Eagles to what seemed like an unstoppable season. Wentz had become a standout performer, putting his team in a great position to make a deep playoff run.

But then, everything changed late in the season. While diving for a touchdown against the Los Angeles Rams, Wentz tore his ACL. The injury ended his season, leaving him on the sidelines as the Eagles chased a championship without him.

This was a tough pill for Wentz to swallow. Instead of leading his team to glory, he had to watch as backup quarterback Nick Foles stepped in, taking the Eagles to victory in the Super Bowl and earning the Super Bowl MVP award. Wentz had worked hard all season, only to see someone else take the spotlight.

But rather than think about what he had lost, Wentz chose to trust in a bigger purpose. He admitted that believing in God's will was hard, especially since it sometimes didn't make sense to him. But by leaning on Scripture, he found peace. He said that Proverbs 16:9 reminded him that while he could make plans, God's direction was always better.

Wentz compared his tough time to gold in a fire. Like gold is heated to remove impurities and improve quality, difficult things such as injuries, losses, or setbacks strengthen and develop us. God uses challenges to shape our character, grow our faith, and guide us toward becoming who He created us to be.

When setbacks hit—whether it's an injury, self-doubt, or lack of motivation—trust that God is working for your good. While it may be hard to understand why these things happen, look for the lessons God is teaching you, and remember He is guiding your steps each day.

PUTTING IT INTO PLAY

What is a recent struggle or setback you've experienced? How could it serve to make you stronger? Keep in mind that the refining process can often lead to your greatest triumphs.

PRAYER

Heavenly Father, thank You for walking through challenges with me. Please help me remember that You are refining me in the fire during hard times. Just as gold becomes better and brighter after being refined, help me trust that You are shaping me for something greater. May I surrender my plans to Yours. Amen.

33

BOLD AS A LION

*The wicked flee though no one pursues, but the righteous
are as bold as a lion.*
Proverbs 28:1

LESSONS FROM THE GAME

What does it mean to stand boldly in your faith? For NBA player Jonathan Isaac, it meant standing—literally—while everyone else knelt.

Isaac, a 6'10" power forward for the Orlando Magic, is known for his strong faith and boldness for Christ. Inspired by his favorite verse, Proverbs 28:1, he strives to live boldly for Jesus on and off the court. Isaac's boldness was put to the test during a 2020 NBA game against the Brooklyn Nets when he made a decision that set him apart.

During the national anthem, players and coaches from both teams knelt to support a social cause surrounding the African American community. Isaac, himself an African American, chose to stand. After the game, reporters pressed him about his decision to stand. He clarified that his choice wasn't against his community but rather a personal conviction that the Gospel was the best way to bring healing and unity.

Isaac explained that true change starts with the heart, and the Gospel, centered on love and unity, offers a better solution. By standing, he wasn't minimizing what his teammates knelt for. Instead, he was pointing to Jesus as the ultimate solution to the challenges and unfairness of today's world.

His decision wasn't easy. It took courage to stand alone, knowing he would be misunderstood. But Isaac's boldness reminds us that following Christ sometimes means making choices that go against the crowd.

Proverbs 28:1 assures us that when we trust in God, we can stand firm with courage—just like a lion.

PUTTING IT INTO PLAY

Have you ever felt unsure about sharing or standing up for your faith? What's one small step you can take to be more bold? It could be inviting a teammate to church or offering to pray for a friend going through a tough time. Ask God for the courage to take that step.

PRAYER

Dear Lord, thank You for the boldness You give
me to stand firm in faith. Please help me live with
the same courage as Jonathan Isaac and choose
what's right, standing for You even when it may be
unpopular or uncomfortable. Amen.

34

STAY GROUNDED

You may say to yourself, "My power and the strength of my hands have produced this wealth for me." But remember the LORD your God, for it is he who gives you the ability to produce wealth, and so confirms his covenant, which he swore to your ancestors, as it is today.
Deuteronomy 8:17-18

LESSONS FROM THE GAME

H er father was an NFL quarterback. Her mother, a professional ballerina. But Vashti Cunningham's biggest influence? Her faith.

At just 26 years old, Vashti Cunningham was one of the world's best high jumpers, representing Team USA in the 2024 Olympics. Her path was shaped by two very different worlds—football and ballet—teaching her to balance power and poise. This unique combination helps her thrive in a sport where every millimeter counts.

But Cunningham doesn't think her success is just about good family genes or natural talent. She's quick to give God credit for everything in her life, saying, "When you see me you see His power. I can't do any of it without His help and guidance." For her, everything she's achieved is a reflection of God's presence in her life, not just her skills or hard work.

Cunningham's humility demonstrates the message of Deuteronomy 8:17-18, which warns against believing that our success is solely the result of our own efforts. While nothing is wrong with being proud of a successful season or big win, we should never forget the true source of our gifts.

God is the one who gives us our talents, opportunities, and strength.

Cunningham trains hard and stays disciplined—but at the end of the day, she knows it's God who has lifted her higher than she could ever go on her own.

PUTTING IT INTO PLAY

Have you ever found yourself taking pride in your accomplishments and forgetting the true source of your abilities? Challenge yourself to shift your focus from personal achievement to gratitude, recognizing that all of your talents are a gift from God.

PRAYER

Dear God, thank You for the blessings You've given me. Remind me that my strength and success come from You, not from my own efforts. Please help me remain humble and grateful, always recognizing Your hand in my achievements. Amen.

35

EYES ON THE PRIZE

Do you not know that in a race all the runners run, but only one gets the prize? Run in such a way as to get the prize. Everyone who competes in the games goes into strict training. They do it to get a crown that will not last, but we do it to get a crown that will last forever.

1 Corinthians 9:24-25

LESSONS FROM THE GAME

Olympic swimmer Michael Phelps didn't just want to win—he wanted to dominate. His training was relentless, and his discipline was unmatched. By the time he retired, he had won 23 Olympic gold medals—more than twice as many as any athlete in history.

Spending 5-6 hours a day in the pool and grinding through high-intensity workouts, Phelps committed to an unforgiving training regimen to reach that level. Even recovery was a test of discipline. Ice baths, stretching, and massages weren't for comfort—they kept him ready to push his limits again the next day.

In 1 Corinthians 9:24-25, the Apostle Paul compares life to a race, reminding us that our goal isn't a medal but something far more worthwhile—eternal life in Heaven. Just as Phelps trained with purpose and commitment, we should pursue spiritual growth with that same drive.

Spiritual training is about getting closer to God. This might involve starting your day with prayer or unplugging from social media to devote more time to Him. It's about being intentional and consistent, just like an athlete training for a competition.

Think about how Phelps spent years preparing for races that lasted only seconds. If he could dedicate so much to something so short-lived, how much more should we devote to something that lasts forever?

PUTTING IT INTO PLAY

You're already taking a step in your spiritual training by reading this devotional. But how can you build on it? This week, challenge yourself to spend a few extra minutes in prayer or reflect on a Bible verse beyond what's in this devotional.

PRAYER

Dear Lord, thank You for allowing me to run this
race of life. Please give me the drive to seek You daily
and the discipline to grow in faith through prayer,
service, and intentional time with You. I want to live
a life that honors You and prepares me for the eternal
prize You have waiting. Amen.

36

UNDER PRESSURE

Do not be anxious about anything, but in every situation, by prayer and petition, with thanksgiving, present your requests to God. And the peace of God, which transcends all understanding, will guard your hearts and your minds in Christ Jesus.
Philippians 4:6-7

LESSONS FROM THE GAME

In 2012, Jeremy Lin, a 24-year-old former point guard from Harvard, was on the verge of being cut from his third NBA team in three years, the struggling New York Knicks.

But then something unforgettable happened: "Linsanity."

After a month on the Knicks' bench, Lin finally got his chance. With the Knicks playing poorly and nothing to lose, the coach put him in. Lin delivered, scoring 25 points and leading a comeback victory.

That night sparked a seven-game winning streak, during which Lin was unstoppable, transforming him from an unknown player into an overnight sensation. The media called the phenomenon *Linsanity*, as fans watched him dominate and shatter expectations.

But with the sudden fame and non-stop media coverage, Lin struggled with intense pre-game anxiety. He feared letting down his teammates, coaches, fans, and family. Despite his outward success, Lin was desperate to find peace.

To manage this pressure, Lin turned to his faith, drawing strength from prayer and Scripture. By leaning on God and concentrating on what he could control—his effort, attitude, and love for the game—Lin felt better prepared to handle the demands of professional basketball.

Pressure is part of the game, but it doesn't have to own you. Today's verse gives us some solid advice: "Do not be anxious about anything." This doesn't mean ignoring problems, but it does mean not letting worry take control.

When the pressure feels heavy, ask God for comfort and guidance. While prayer isn't a magic fix that makes problems disappear, it connects you with God, who can give you the strength and peace to overcome your worries.

PUTTING IT INTO PLAY

Feeling pressure in school, sports, or other parts of your life? Take a moment to pray—tell God what's on your mind and ask Him for peace. Focus on what you can control and trust Him with the rest.

PRAYER

Heavenly Father, thank You for being with me in moments of pressure and uncertainty. When I feel overwhelmed, please help me pause and turn to You, trusting that Your peace will guard my heart and mind. Amen.

37

ROOTED IN FAITH

But blessed is the one who trusts in the LORD, whose confidence is in him. They will be like a tree planted by the water that sends out its roots by the stream. It does not fear when heat comes; its leaves are always green. It has no worries in a year of drought and never fails to bear fruit.
Jeremiah 17:7-8

LESSONS FROM THE GAME

Tom Brady took the snap, glanced downfield, and fired the ball without hesitation. He already knew where Rob Gronkowski would be.

Brady and Gronkowski were one of the NFL's most electrifying partnerships, connecting for 90 touchdowns—more than any quarterback-tight end duo in history—and winning four Super Bowl rings together. But their success wasn't just about skill. It was built on deep trust from over a decade of playing together.

Brady didn't just throw and hope. He trusted Gronkowski to be exactly where he needed to be. Gronkowski, in turn, trusted Brady to put the ball in the right spot. Whether in the first quarter or the final seconds of a game, their confidence in each other never wavered. This relationship helped them deliver under pressure and execute when it mattered most.

That kind of trust changes everything—in sports and faith. When we trust God, we don't have to see the whole picture to know He's leading us. We can be confident that He is always working for our good, even when we can't see the outcome. Letting go of worry and trusting God's plan frees us from anxiety and gives us the strength to face challenges without fear.

Like the tree in today's verse, when its roots are deep and connected to water, it remains strong and fruitful, even in a drought. With deep faith roots, we can stand firm and keep growing—no matter what life throws our way.

PUTTING IT INTO PLAY

Has anything been stressing you out lately? Take a moment to talk with God about it and trust Him to take care of the outcome. Let go of trying to fix everything yourself and ask God to fill your heart with His peace instead.

PRAYER

Dear God, like a tree with deep roots, help me stay grounded in You. Teach me to trust Your guidance and let go of control. Please fill my heart with peace, replacing my anxiety with faith. Amen.

38

STAY COACHABLE

Stop listening to instruction, my son, and you will stray from the words of knowledge.
Proverbs 19:27

LESSONS FROM THE GAME

With 24 Grand Slam titles, Novak Djokovic stands among tennis's greatest legends.

But despite his dominance, he never relies solely on his own knowledge. Djokovic actively seeks wisdom—whether it's refining his technique with world-class coaches, consulting sports psychologists, or adopting cutting-edge training methods. His willingness to learn and adapt helps keep him ahead of the competition.

Djokovic's mindset reflects Proverbs 19:27—true growth comes from continually seeking wisdom. If the greatest tennis player in the world depends on expert guidance to improve, how much more should we seek wisdom to navigate our lives?

Success can sometimes make us think we've figured it all out. But when we stop listening to wisdom, we can develop blind spots that hold us back. Refusing to take advice leads to avoidable mistakes and missed opportunities for growth.

Thankfully, we have access to the ultimate source of wisdom: the Bible. God's Word provides the guidance we need to face challenges, make wise decisions, and grow in character. God also places mentors in our lives—coaches, teachers, parents, and spiritual leaders—to help us apply His teachings.

To keep growing—athletically or spiritually—we must stay coachable. Stay humble, keep learning, and trust that God is shaping you into the best version of yourself.

PUTTING IT INTO PLAY

How did you react the last time you received constructive feedback? Did you get defensive? Or did you humbly accept it and take action? Think about how humility and opening your heart and mind to new perspectives could help you improve.

PRAYER

Dear Lord, thank You for the guidance available to me through Your Word. Help me turn to the Bible for wisdom and remain open to the support of godly mentors You place in my life. Please keep my heart coachable and my mind open. Amen.

39

MASTERING THE FUNDAMENTALS

Therefore everyone who hears these words of mine and puts them into practice is like a wise man who built his house on the rock.
Matthew 7:24

LESSONS FROM THE GAME

Stephen Curry didn't become one of the greatest shooters in NBA history by chasing highlight plays—he built his success on the basics.

Curry has gone viral for his pregame drills, where you'll see him laser-focused on simple yet powerful skills like dribbling, passing, and layups. His relentless attention to the fundamentals allows him to perform at the highest level, night after night.

Similar to how mastering basketball fundamentals helps Curry perform under pressure, building a solid faith foundation prepares us for life's challenges. This happens when we focus on spiritual "reps" like reading the Bible and praying regularly.

So, how does this work in real life? When Scripture is part of your routine, you'll have a collection of truths in your mind to pull from. If stress hits, you'll be able to recall verses like 1 Peter 5:7: "Cast all your anxiety on him because he cares for you." Because you've stored God's Word in your heart, you'll have the wisdom and comfort you need—right when you need it.

It's easy to overlook the basics, whether in sports or faith. As an athlete, you might want to skip drills and go straight for the big plays. As a Christian, you might feel tempted to skip prayer or reading the Bible. But just as nailing the basics in sports gets you ready for the big moments, building a solid spiritual foundation prepares you to tackle life's challenges with strength and confidence.

PUTTING IT INTO PLAY

Do you make time to pray or read God's Word, or have you skipped these basics? Remember, strengthening the fundamentals is key to a strong relationship with God. What's one small way you can commit to these foundations this week?

PRAYER

Dear God, please help me devote myself to the basics of my faith. Strengthen me to build a solid foundation with You so I can stand firm in all that comes my way. I trust You will meet me where I am and help me grow. Amen.

40

SPEAK LIFE

Do not let any unwholesome talk come out of your mouths, but only what is helpful for building others up according to their needs, that it may benefit those who listen.
Ephesians 4:29

LESSONS FROM THE GAME

When you picture an NFL defensive lineman, you might think of a powerful, imposing football player—loud, intense, and probably using language that wouldn't fly in church.

But not all of them fit that stereotype.

Gerald McCoy, a six-time Pro Bowl defensive tackle, chose a different path. While many players let loose with profanity on the field and in the locker room, McCoy committed not to. McCoy has said, "We speak life into a lot of things with the language we use." McCoy knows that what we say matters, so he uses his words to encourage, inspire, and reflect the love of Jesus.

Now retired from professional football, McCoy uses his platform as a sports analyst and commentator to share positivity with his audience. Whether on TV, in person, or online, he intentionally uses communication—both spoken and written—to build others up.

Ephesians 4:29 reminds us that our words have power. What we say can fuel drama or bring peace. Our words can inspire and encourage, or they can create division and hurt.

As student-athletes, we're often surrounded by negative language. It can be heard in the locker room, on the playing field, in social media posts, or even from coaches in heated moments. Over time, these words can slip into our conversations and vocabulary.

But as followers of Christ, we are called to be different—to use our words in a way that points back to Jesus.

Jesus said our words reveal what's in our hearts. When we let God shape our hearts, our words will reflect His love—building others up instead of tearing them down.

PUTTING IT INTO PLAY

Think about the words you've been using in person and online lately. Do they encourage others, or do they tear people down? This week, before you speak or type, challenge yourself to add more positivity to what you say.

PRAYER

Dear Jesus, I thank You for the ability to speak and connect with others. Help me choose my words carefully so they may honor You and encourage those around me. When I fall short, forgive and guide me to speak with love. Amen.

BEYOND THE GAME

The last 40 days weren't just about sports. They were about something deeper—how faith molds who you are.

You've read stories of athletes facing challenges and seen how relying on God builds strength that lasts.

As you move forward, don't leave Scripture behind. It shapes how you think, how you make choices, and how you handle pressure. The more you stay connected to God through prayer and His Word, the more steady and confident you'll be—no matter what comes next.

Sports won't last forever, but your faith will. When God is at the center, playing isn't just about the scoreboard—it's about who you represent. The effort you bring, the attitude you show, and the way you treat others all speak louder than any win ever could.

So go after excellence. Play with heart. And above all, compete in a way that reflects the One you play for.